Boa Constrictors

By Sam Dollar

Raintree

ANIMALS OF THE RAINFOREST

www.raintreepublishers.co.uk
Visit our website to find out more information about Raintree books.

To order:
☎ Phone 44 (0) 1865 888112
📄 Send a fax to 44 (0) 1865 314091
💻 Visit the Raintree Bookshop at www.raintreepublishers.co.uk to browse our catalogue and order online.

First published in Great Britain by Raintree Publishers, Halley Court, Jordan Hill, Oxford, OX2 8EJ, part of Harcourt Education.
Raintree is a registered trademark of Harcourt Education Ltd.

Originated by Dot Gradations Ltd
Printed and bound in Hong Kong and China by South China

ISBN 1 844 21090 1
07 06 05 04 03
10 9 8 7 6 5 4 3 2 1

British Library Cataloguing in Publication Data
Dollar, Sam
Boa constrictors - (Animals of the rainforest)
1. Boa constrictor - Juvenile literature
2. Rain forest ecology - Juvenile literature
I.Title
597.9'6
A catalogue for this book is available from the British Library.

Acknowledgements
The publishers would like to thank the following for permission to reproduce photographs:
Corbis, pp. **16, 19, 20, 22**; Visuals Unlimited/Joe McDonald, pp. **1, 4–5, 8, 11, 24**; Jim Merli, pp. **12, 14**; John Cunningham, **26**; W. Ormerod, **28**; Warren Photographic, pp. **7, 13, 17**.

Cover photograph by Nature Picture Library/Mary McDonald.

Every effort has been made to contact copyright holders of any material reproduced in this book. Any omissions will be rectified in subsequent printings if notice is given to the publishers.

Contents

Any words appearing in the text in bold, **like this**, are explained in the Glossary.

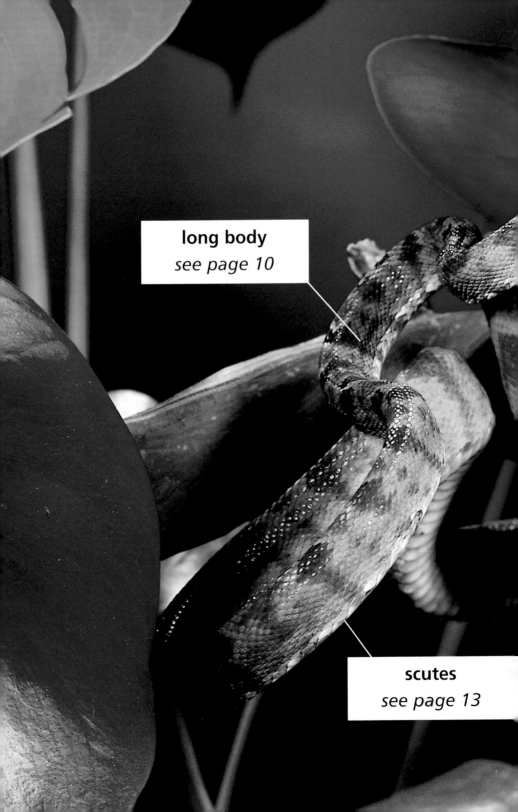

long body
see page 10

scutes
see page 13

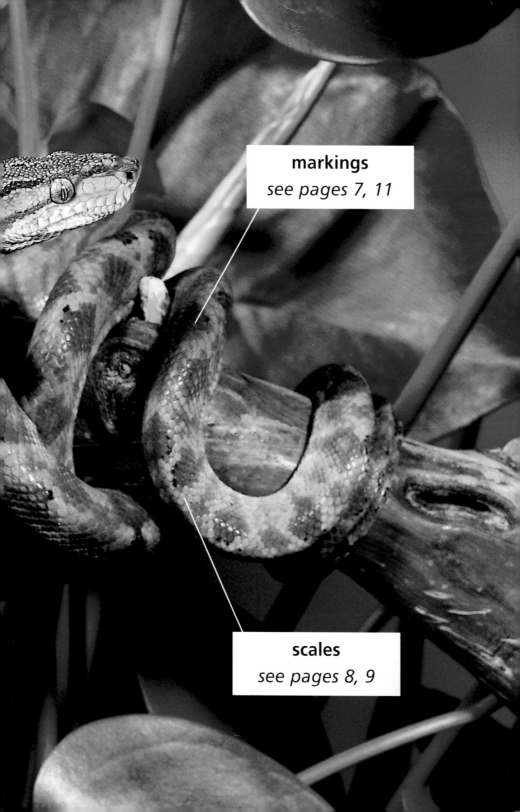

markings
see pages 7, 11

scales
see pages 8, 9

USA

MEXICO

BELIZE
GUATEMALA   HONDURAS
EL SALVADOR   NICARAGUA
COSTA RICA
PANAMA

Caribbean Sea

North Atlantic
Ocean

VENEZUELA
GUYANA   SURINAM
FRENCH GUIANA
COLOMBIA

ECUADOR

Amazon River

PERU

BRAZIL

BOLIVIA

PARAGUAY

South Pacific
Ocean

URUGUAY

ARGENTINA

CHILE

South Atlantic
Ocean

Range of the boa constrictor
Surrounding land
Sea
Borders
Rivers

6

A quick look at boa constrictors

What do boa constrictors look like?

Boa constrictors are brown, red, grey or cream coloured snakes. They have dark brown to deep red-brown markings. A marking is a pattern on an animal. The markings get wider and darker near the tail.

Where do boa constrictors live?

Many boa constrictors live in the Central and South American rainforests. They also live in Mexico and Argentina.

What do boa constrictors eat?

Boa constrictors eat other animals. They eat lizards, rats, mice, pigs, squirrels and birds. Larger boa constrictors may eat small deer.

This is a close-up view of a boa constrictor's scales.

About boa constrictors

Boa constrictors are **reptiles**. A reptile is a **cold-blooded** animal. The blood in cold-blooded animals warms or cools to about the same temperature as the air or water around them. Temperature is a measure of heat or cold. Boa constrictors warm their bodies by lying in the sun. They cool their bodies by lying in the shade.

Tough **scales** cover boa constrictors' bodies like on all reptiles. Scales are small flaps of hard skin that overlap each other. They are made out of a material called **keratin**. People's fingernails are made of the same material as a boa constrictor's scales.

Where boa constrictors live

Boa constrictors live in different **habitats**. A habitat is a place where an animal or plant usually lives. Some boa constrictors live in dry parts of Mexico and Argentina. Many live in the rainforests of South and Central America. Rainforests are places where many trees and plants grow close together and lots of rain falls. The Amazon rainforest is the largest rainforest in the world. It grows around the river Amazon in South America. Many different kinds of animals live in rainforests.

Boa constrictors live in different places in the rainforest. Young boa constrictors climb trees. Adult boa constrictors crawl along the ground. They also spend time near rivers and streams.

What boa constrictors look like

Boa constrictors are large snakes. Females grow larger than males. The average boa constrictor adult is from 1.8 to 3.4 metres long. It weighs about 13.6 kilograms.

This boa constrictor is crawling out of a river in the rainforest.

Boa constrictors are cream, brown, red or grey coloured with dark brown markings. A marking is a pattern on an animal. The markings get wider and darker towards the tail.

Over time, boa constrictors have changed to fit in with their environment.

Crawling

Boa constrictors use large scales called **scutes** to travel on land. Scutes cover the underside of boa constrictors. The snakes push and pull themselves along by pressing the scutes into the ground.

Boa constrictors also have **spurs**. Spurs are small bones that stick out near their tails. They are like claws. Scientists think these spurs are what is left of leg bones. They think that boa constrictors may once have had legs.

Boa constrictor skeletons have bones that look like pelvis bones and leg bones. Scientists think these bones show that boa constrictors have changed over time. The scientists think the boa constrictors changed as their environment changed. This helped them survive better in changing habitats.

Some boa constrictors open their mouths when they are about to attack.

Hunting and eating

Boa constrictors are carnivores. Carnivores are animals that eat only other animals. Boa constrictors eat lizards, rats, mice, pigs, squirrels and birds. Larger boa constrictors will eat small deer and ocelots. Ocelots are small, spotted wild cats that also live in the rainforest.

Boa constrictors can live a long time without food. Large boa constrictors can go months between meals. This is helpful when food is difficult to find.

Hunting

Boa constrictors are **predators**. Predators are
animals that eat other animals. The animals that
predators eat are called prey. Boa constrictors
often wait quietly in trees or bushes for prey.
They blend in with the trees and grass, so they
are difficult to see.

Boa constrictors sometimes sneak up on prey. They will climb trees to catch birds or other animals. They will crawl into holes in the ground to find prey.

A boa constrictor strikes when it finds prey. Striking means it shoots forwards with its mouth open. Then it sinks its teeth into the prey. It wraps its body around the animal while its teeth hold the prey.

Boa constrictors' teeth curve backwards to stop prey from escaping. The teeth sink deeper into the prey if it tries to get free.

Boa constrictors kill their prey by squeezing tightly. They hold prey so tight that it cannot breathe. The prey's blood stops flowing. After a few minutes, it dies.

Many people say that boa constrictors crush the bones of their prey. This is not true. They squeeze only hard enough to stop the prey from breathing.

Eating

Boa constrictors have special jaws that open very wide. They swallow their prey whole. In the roof of a boa constrictor's mouth is a group of **cells** called **Jacobson's organ**. A cell is a small part of an animal or plant. Boa constrictors press their tongues against Jacobson's organ to help them smell and taste.

Swallowing large prey takes a long time. The boa constrictor's mouth slowly works its way around the prey. Then muscles inside the throat grip the prey. These muscles push the prey to the stomach.

Strong stomach juices help boa constrictors digest bones and beaks of prey. To digest is to break down food so the body can use it. A small lizard can be digested in a few days. A larger animal can take more than two weeks to digest. You can see a lump in a boa constrictor's body when it has swallowed an animal. The lump stays there until the prey breaks down.

Boa constrictors open their mouths wide to swallow prey.

The outside temperature controls how fast a boa constrictor can break down food. The boa constrictor breaks down food more slowly in cool weather. That is why it might have to lie in the sun after eating, to warm up. The heat helps it break down food faster.

Boa constrictors spend most of their lives on their own.

A boa constrictor's life cycle

Boa constrictors mate once a year. They live alone and come together only during the mating season. Females give off special scents to attract males. After mating, the male boa constrictor goes off on his own.

Female boa constrictors do not lay eggs like most reptiles. The young grow inside the female for six to ten months. Then females give birth to mature young. Large female boa constrictors give birth to up to fifty young at a time.

> **This adult boa constrictor has few enemies in its natural habitat.**

Egg sac

A thin and clear egg sac covers newly born boa constrictors. A sac is an animal or plant part that is shaped like a bag. Most young boa constrictors break through the sac easily. They will die if they cannot break out.

Young boa constrictors can be up to 60 centimetres long at birth. The length of young boa constrictors depends largely on the length of the mother. Longer females usually give birth to longer young.

On their own

Female boa constrictors leave their young immediately after they are born. Young boa constrictors must care for themselves. They have to hunt for food. They must hide from predators without the help of their mothers.

Only a few boa constrictors will become adults. Many die after a few weeks because birds, wild pigs and other snakes eat them. When they are young, they are not large enough or strong enough to fight back. If they grow larger, they will have few enemies.

This is the shed skin of a boa constrictor after moulting.

Moulting

Like all snakes, a boa constrictor gets too big for its skin as it grows. New skin begins to grow underneath the old skin. The snakes shed their old skins when they grow. This is called **moulting**.

Moulting begins when a boa constrictor's new skin underneath is fully grown. It may rub against a rock to help loosen the old skin. The old skin peels back as the snake crawls out of it.

Boa constrictors continue to grow throughout their lives. As they grow, they have to moult again and again. Boa constrictors can live for 30 to 40 years.

This is an ancient Aztec statue of a boa constrictor.

Life with boa constrictors

In early times, the Aztec and Maya Indians of Central America believed boa constrictors and other snakes were gods. They thought these snakes could help bring rain for their crops. They carved huge boa constrictors out of stone to honour the snakes.

Christopher Columbus landed in the West Indies in 1492. He and his explorers went back to England and told stories of giant monsters. They said these monsters were hundreds of metres long and could swallow elephants. They did not know that what they had seen were boa constrictors and other large snakes.

> Some people keep a boa constrictor as a pet. But boa constrictors need special care.

Stories

People no longer ask boa constrictors to help bring rain, but they still tell stories about them. One of these stories is that boa constrictors crawl faster than a person can run. This is not true. Boa constrictors move slowly. Another story is that boa constrictors kill and swallow many people each year. This also is not true. They do not grow large enough to eat people.

Boa constrictors as pets

Boa constrictors are sometimes kept as pets. They are very quiet and like to stay still much of the time. They do not make noises. They do not need to be fed very often. But they have to be given other special care or they will become ill.

Owners of boa constrictors need to be careful. Many large boa constrictors will strike at any sudden movement. They can eat cats and dogs. Owners of boa constrictors can be bitten.

In the wild

There are many boa constrictors living in the wild. They are not listed as endangered. Endangered means in danger of dying out.

People who buy and sell boa constrictors as pets must obey laws about catching and delivering the animals. Without laws, the buying and selling of boa constrictors would probably increase. The laws help make sure that boa constrictors will not die out. They also help to make sure the animals are looked after properly.

Glossary

cell building blocks of an animal or plant

cold-blooded animals with blood that warms or cools to about the same temperature as the air or water around them

habitat place where an animal or plant usually lives

Jacobson's organ (JAYK-ub-suns OR-gun) group of cells in a snake's mouth that helps it taste and smell

keratin strong, flexible substance found in body parts such as scales, fingernails and hooves

moult to shed an outer skin or covering

predator animal that hunts other animals

reptile cold-blooded animal that crawls or creeps

scales overlapping flaps of thick, hard skin that cover an animal's body

scutes large scales on a snake's underside, which it uses to pull itself along

spurs tiny bones that stick out either side of the base of a boa constrictor's tail, probably left over from when boas had legs

More information

Internet sites

Rainforest Concern
www.rainforestconcern.org

World Wide Fund for Nature
www.panda.org

Useful address

World Wildlife Fund-UK
Panda House, Weyside Park
Godalming, Surrey, GU7 1XR

Books to read

Miles, Elizabeth. *Why do animals have skin and scales?* Heinemann Library, Oxford, 2002.

Robinson, Claire. *Really wild: Snake*. Heinemann Library, Oxford, 2000.

Index